Mike Bartlett

Artefacts

T0258370

B L O O M S B U R Y

LONDON • NEW DELHI • NEW YORK • SYDNEY

Bloomsbury Methuen Drama

An imprint of Bloomsbury Publishing Plc

50 Bedford Square	1385 Broadway
London	New York
WC1B 3DP	NY 10018
UK	USA

www.bloomsbury.com

Bloomsbury is a registered trade mark of Bloomsbury Publishing Plc

Published by Methuen Drama 2008

Visit www.bloomsbury.com to find out more about our authors and their books
You will find extracts, author interviews, author events and you can sign up for newsletters to be the first to hear about our latest releases and special offers.

British Library Cataloguing-in-Publication Data
A catalogue record for this book is available from the British Library.

ISBN: PB: 978-1-4081-0677-8
        ePDF: 978-1-4081-0997-7
        ePUB: 978-1-4081-4194-6

Library of Congress Cataloging-in-Publication Data
A catalog record for this book is available from the Library of Congress.

nabokov

thebushtheatre

nabokov

in association with
The Bush Theatre
presents the world premiere of

Artefacts

by Mike Bartlett

25 February – 22 March 2008

Cast

Kelly	**Lizzy Watts**
Susan	**Karen Ascoe**
Ibrahim	**Peter Polycarpou**
Faiza	**Mouna Albakry**
Raya	**Amy Hamdoon**

Directed by	**James Grieve**
Designed by	**Lucy Osborne**
Lighting Designed by	**Hartley T A Kemp**
Music composed by	**Arthur Darvill**
Assistant director	**Tara Wilkinson**
Production Manager (London)	**Ric Mountjoy**
Production Manager (Tour)	**Nick Fieldsend**
Company Stage Manager	**Jess Gow**
Dialect Coach	**Michaela Kennan**
Producer	**Emma Brunjes**

Artefacts was first performed at The Bush Theatre, London, on 25 February 2008.

Artefacts is produced in association with Old Vic New Voices and is made possible by a Stage One/Society of London Theatre New Producer's Bursary sponsored by FIFA (Federation Internationale des Football Associations), in association with MAMMA MIA! and Arts Council England, and supported by the Mackintosh Foundation, the Wingate Foundation, Live Nation, Andrew Treagus Associates, The Underwood Trust and Equity Trust.

nabokov would like to thank: Josie Rourke, Christabel Anderson, Angela Bond, Fiona Clark, Abigail Gonda, Bob Holmes, Anthea Williams and all at The Bush; Kate Pakenham, Tiffany Nesbitt, Rachael Stevens, Steve Winter and all at Old Vic New Voices; Auro and Jack Foxcroft at Village Underground; Chloe Emmerson; Juliet Horsley; Kai Chan Vong; Nick Salmon and Natasha Ockrent at Stage One / SOLT New Producers' Award; Mark Rubinstein; Tim Roseman and Paul Robinson; John Davidson, Roger McCann and all at Arts Council England, East; Sebastian Warrack; Roxana Silbert and all at Paines Plough; Brigid Larmour and all at Watford Palace Theatre; Hassan Abdulrazzak; Louise Hillmand at Ken McReddie; Helen Seagriff at Feast Management; Sophie Hirst at Daly Pearson; Claire Vidal-Hall; West Central Management; Nick Quinn at The Agency; Jeffrey Cambell.

And all the actors who have helped with the development of the script:
Myanna Buring, Joanne Howarth, Stephanie Leonidas, Lois Norman, Farzana Dua Elahe, Soumaya Mossen, Amerjit Deu, Naomi Wattis, Shelley Islam, Victoria Jeffrey, Hajaz Akram, Tiran Aakel, Jenny Gleave, Elizabeth Edmonds, Sara Bahadori.

Artefacts is produced in association with Old Vic New Voices and is supported by a Stage One/SOLT New Producers' Bursary.

The National Tour of Artefacts is supported by Arts Council England, East.

nabokov

"Proving that political drama does have a place in the 21st Century" *The List*

nabokov is a new writing theatre company dedicated to commissioning, developing and producing backlash theatre – new work that offers an antagonistic response to contemporary agendas, trends and events.

Since 2001, we have produced critically acclaimed productions in London, Edinburgh and on tour, including KITCHEN, BEDTIME FOR BASTARDS, CAMARILLA and NIKOLINA. Our World Premiere production of TERRE HAUTE by Edmund White premiered at The Assembly Rooms, Edinburgh, in August 2006 prior to a National Tour and West End run at Trafalgar Studios in 2007.

We aim to develop new work through events, workshops, readings and literary programmes. Our monthly development forum, SHORTS, ran for five years in Sheffield, Manchester, Liverpool and London, offering cross-disciplinary artists the chance to test out new work in front of an audience. Our PRESENT : TENSE events challenge playwrights to write plays in response to the most important story on the news agenda in just one week.

ARTEFACTS is our latest commission. It was awarded the inaugural Old Vic New Voices Award for new writing and a Stage One / Society of London Theatres New Producer's Bursary.

nabokov and the National Tour of ARTEFACTS are generously supported by Arts Council England, East.

For **nabokov**:

Artistic Directors	**James Grieve and George Perrin**
Executive Director	**Ric Mountjoy**
Associate Producer	**Emma Brunjes**
Administrator	**Sally Christopher**
Playwright-In-Residence	**Joel Horwood**

hello@nabokov-online.com // www.nabokov-online.com

Artefacts

National Tour 2007

25 February-22 March
The Bush Theatre, London
☎ (020) 7602 3703

26 - 27 March
Emlyn Williams Theatre, Theatre Clwyd
☎ (0845) 330 3565

7 - 8 April
The McCarthy Studio, Stephen Joseph Theatre, Scarborough
☎ (01723) 370 541

10 - 12 April
Ustinov Studio, Bath Theatre Royal
☎ (01225) 448 844

23 – 24 April
Salberg Studio, Salisbury Playhouse
☎ (01722) 320 333

30 April
Norwich Playhouse
☎ (01603) 598 598

1 – 2 May
Mercury Theatre, Colchester
☎ (01206) 573 948

6 – 10 May
Drum Theatre Plymouth
☎ (01752) 267 222

Mike Bartlett Writer

Plays include *My Child* (Royal Court), *Contractions* (Royal Court - forthcoming).

Adaptations include *The Lesson* (Arcola). Radio includes *Love Contract* (Radio 4), *The Family Man* (Radio 4), *Not Talking* (Radio 3).

He is currently Pearson Playwright in Residence at The Royal Court Theatre. He won the Writer's Guild Tinniswood and Imison prizes for *Not Talking*, and the Old Vic New Voices Award for *Artefacts*.

The Company

Mouna Albakry (Faiza)

Mouna grew up in the US, France, Sultanate of Oman, Kenya and the UK picking up four languages along the way. Her first time on stage was during a French high school production of *Le Petit Prince* in Paris. Theatre includes *Ten Dollar Drinks*, *Wanda's Visit* (Courtyard Theatre) and *The Wedding Party* (Union Theatre).

Radio and voiceover credits include Marcus Brigstocke's *Giles Wemmbley Hogg Goes Off (to Tanzania)*, *Sand* (BBC), *Baghdad's Burning* (BBC), *Rome Interactive CDX* (BBC Online), *World of Primary Learning - Challenging Perceptions (Palestine)* (Qualifications and Curriculum Authority) and Mrs. Ibrahim in Ben Bolt's *Second Nature* with Alec Baldwin.

Karen Ascoe (Susan)

Theatre in London includes *The Letter* (Wyndhams), *A Shayna Maidel* (Ambassadors), *Ivanov* and *Much Ado About Nothing* (Strand), *Anna Karenina* for Shared Experience (Lyric Hammersmith, Tricycle and International tours), *Out There* (Riverside studios), *Three Viewings* (New End). For the Orange Tree Theatre: *The Years Between*, *The Cassilis Engagement*, *Silas Marner*, *Dr. Knock*, *The Case of Rebellious Susan*, *Pere Goriot*, and the original production of Geoffrey Beevers' award-winning *Adam Bede*. Other theatre credits include the UK tour of *The Shell Seekers*, *After Mrs. Rochester* for Shared Experience (UK and International tour), *Tartuffe*, *Hay Fever* (Haymarket, Basingstoke), *Perfect Days*, *Time of My Life*, *Extremities* (Playhouse, Derby), *Taking Steps*, *Season's Greetings* (Sonning), *Rookery Nook*, *Twelfth Night*, *The Rivals* (Mercury, Colchester), *Loot* and *The Glass Menagerie* (Swan, Worcester).

Recent television work includes *Eastenders*, *Doctors*, *Beethoven*, *The Bill*, *Dream Team*, *Casualty*, *Armadillo*, *The Armando Iannucci Shows*, *London's Burning*, *Peak Practice*, *Kid in The Corner*.

Film includes *Paper Mask*, *Loaf*.

While training at the Guildhall School of Music & Drama, Karen won the BBC Carleton Hobbs Award and so spent 7 months with the Radio Drama Company. Favourite parts include Dorine in *Tartuffe* and Miranda in *The Tempest* with the late Sir John Gielgud.

Emma Brunjes (Producer)

Emma is Head of Avalon Promotions for whom she has most recently produced and promoted *Frank Skinner* (UK Tour) *Al Murray - The Pub Landlord* (UK Tour) *Grumpy Old Women -Live* (UK & Australia Tour) *Lee Mack Live* (UK Tour) *Russell Howard* (UK Tour) *Jenny Éclair* (UK Tour.) Emma also produces all Avalon's shows at the Edinburgh Festival, amounting to 21 shows in 2007. Emma's career started at Avalon in the marketing team working on *Jerry Springer - the Opera* (West End & UK Tour.) Her association with nabokov stems from work on *Old Vic New Voices: Starbucks 24 Hour Plays.* Emma is the co-founder and Executive Producer for Deckchair Productions, an independent theatre and film company.

Arthur Darvill (Composer)

Arthur has composed music for various theatre projects including: *Stoopud Fucken Animals* by Joel Horwood for the Traverse Theatre, Edinburgh; *Crazy Love* by Che Walker for Paines Plough; *Suddenly Last Summer*, *The Dolls House* and *Timon of Athens* for RADA; *Drywrite presents: Lyrics* for Drywrite and *Adult Child, Dead Child* for Stage 2 at the Crescent theatre in Birmingham. Arthur is currently working on two projects in collaboration with Che Walker: *Been so Long the Musical* which will receive a public reading at the Soho Theatre in the spring and *The Frontline*, which will have a full production at the Globe in the autumn.

James Grieve (Director)

James trained as assistant and associate director to Josie Rourke on *The Long & The Short & The Tall* (Lyceum, Sheffield) and *Flight Without End* (LAMDA); as staff director to Howard Davies on *Philistines* and *Present Laughter* at The National Theatre; and on the National Theatre Studio Director's Course.

James is co-founder and artistic director of nabokov for whom he has directed and produced *Kitchen* at Sheffield Crucible Studio and Edinburgh Fringe; *Bedtime For Bastards* at the Old Red Lion and Edinburgh Fringe; *Nikolina* at the Edinburgh Fringe and on tour. He produced *Terre Haute* at the Assembly Rooms, on tour and West End and *Camarilla* at the Old Red Lion and Edinburgh Fringe.

As a freelance director James's credits include *Luke Wright: Poet & Man* and *Luke Wright: Poet Laureate* (Pleasance, Edinburgh and on tour); *Simon Brodkin: One Man Comedy Club* and *Everyone But Himself* (Avalon) and *Comfort* by Mike Bartlett as part of the Old Vic's 24 Hour Plays.

Amy Hamdoon (Raya)

Amy trained at Guildford School of Acting.

Theatre whilst training includes *The Two Gentlemen of Verona, The Oresteia, The Beau Defeated* and *Tapestry*.

Theatre since graduating includes understudying all the female roles for Creation Theatre Company's Summer Season of *Hamlet, The Taming of the Shrew* and *The Oxford Passion*. Amy also appeared as chorus and worked as dance captain in *The Oxford Passion*.

Hartley T A Kemp (Lighting Designer)

Previous work at the Bush: *How to Curse*. Other recent theatre includes: *Gaslight* (Old Vic), *The Voysey Inheritance, Elmina's Kitchen, Scenes from the Big Picture* (National); *Romeo and Juliet, The Merry Wives of Windsor, Coriolanus* (RSC); *Kiss of the Spider Woman, Days of Wine and Roses, Passion Play, Good* (Donmar); *Mrs Warren's Profession* (Strand); *The York Realist* (English Touring Theatre/Royal Court), *Faith* (Royal Court); *Great Expectations, American Buffalo* (Gate, Dublin); *Nakamitsu* (Gate, London); *Metamorphosis* (Lyric Hammersmith); *The Field* (Tricycle); *The Rubenstein Kiss* (Hampstead); *Certain Young Men, The Doctor's Dilemma, Tongue of a Bird* (Almeida); *The Birthday Party* (Birmingham Rep), *Arcadia, The Rivals, Loot, Paradise Lost, The Comedy of Errors, The Caretaker* (Bristol Old Vic); *A Number, Gladiator Games, A Midsummer Night's Dream, Original Sin, The Tempest, Don Juan, The Country Wife, A View From the Bridge, As You Like It, Twelfth Night* (Sheffield); *Rutherford and Son* (Royal Exchange, Manchester), *Where There's a Will* (Theatre Royal Bath); *Treehouses* (Northcott, Exeter); *Dealer's Choice* (Clwyd Teatr Cymru); *Dealer's Choice* (West Yorkshire Playhouse)

Musicals include: *Miss Saigon* (Gothenburg); *Showboat, West Side Story* (Innsbruck); *Promises, Promises* (Sheffield); *The Wizard of Oz* (Birmingham Rep).

Opera includes: *Les Pêcheurs des Perles, Iris* (Holland Park); *Mary Seacole, Oreste, Oresteia* (Linbury); *M Butterfly, Martha, The Barber of Seville, La Sonnambula, Carmen* (Castleward). Hartley is also Artistic Director of C venues at the Edinburgh Fringe.

Ric Mountjoy (Production Manager)

Ric is a freelance Production Manager, Lighting Designer and Theatrical Electrician, most recently working with English National Opera and Birmingham Royal Ballet, and also as Chief Electrician of the National Student Drama Festival. Recent credits include Production Management of *1139 Miles*, a devised performance in a found space in Bradford; Lighting Design for *The Swing Left* (Unlimited Theatre) and various National Tours for Small Change Theatre. Ric is a founding member and Executive Director of nabokov, having worked on all their productions since 2002.

Lucy Osborne (Designer)

Lucy graduated from the Motley Theatre Design School.

Theatre for The Bush includes *The dYsFUnCKshOnalZ*. Other theatre credits include *Some Kind of Bliss* (Trafalgar Studios), *Rope (*Watermill Theatre), *Closer* (Northampton Theatre Royal), *Touch Wood* (Stephen Joseph Theatre), *Breaker Morant* (Edinburgh Festival 2007), *Ship of Fools* (set, Theatre 503), *The Long and the Short and the Tall* (Sheffield Lyceum and Tour), *Dr Faustus* (The Place), *Richard III* (Cambridge Arts Theatre), *The Tempest* (set, Box Clever national tour), *The Prayer Room* (Edinburgh International Festival and Birmingham Rep), *Flight Without End, Othello, Lysistrata* (LAMDA), *Season of Migration to the North* (RSC New Work Festival), *Almost Blue,* winner of the Oxford Samuel Beckett Trust Award (Riverside Studios), *The Unthinkable* (Sheffield Crucible Studio) and *Generation* (Gate Theatre, Notting Hill). Forthcoming projects include *Be My Baby* (New Vic Theatre, Stoke).

Peter Polycarpou (Ibrahim)

Theatre includes Gash in *Last Easter* (Birmingham Rep), *Angels in America* (RSC and Aldwych) *Imagine This* (Theatre Royal Plymouth) *Silver Birch House* (Arcola), *Phantom of the Opera* (Her Majesty's Theatre), *Miss Saigon* (Theatre Royal Drury Lane), *Titus Andronicus*, *The Jew of Malta*, *A Question of Geography,* and *The New Inn* (RSC), *Oklahoma* (National Theatre and Lyceum), *Gizmo Love* (Tour), *Anna in the Tropics* (Hampstead), *Follow My Leader* (Hampstead and Birmingham Rep), *They're Playing our Song*, *The Resistible Rise of Arturo Ui* and *The Happy End* (Bridewell), *Les Miserables* (Palace, Barbican RSC, Original Company), *The Heidi Chronicles* (Greenwich), *Frankly Scarlett* (King's Head), *Laughter on the 23rd Floor* (National Tour), *The Secret Garden* (RSC and Aldwych), *The Odd Couple* (Library, Manchester), *The Woods (*Finborough) and *Chitty Chitty Bang Bang* (London Palladium).

Television includes *Birds of a Feather* (BBC), *Holby City* (BBC), *The Bill* (ITV), *Sunburn* (BBC), *American Voices* (BBC), *Mile High* (Sky), *Waking the Dead* (BBC) and *Eastenders* (BBC).

Film includes *Evita* (Hollywood), *Oklahoma* (Umbrella), *De-Lovely* (MGM), *Oh Jerusalem*, *Broken*, *Mad George*.

Radio includes *Sherlock Holmes*, *Murder on the Orient Express*, *Macrunes Guevera*, *It's all Greek to Me*, *Young Gifted and Greek* and *The Brox*.

Lizzy Watts (Kelly)

Lizzy trained at the Royal Welsh College of Music and Drama, graduating in 2006.

Theatre whilst training includes *Tartuffe, The Country Wife, StreetScene, Stars in the Morning Sky, The Art of Success, The Rover* and *Twelfth Night.* Other theatre includes *Bianco* (Elan Productions) *The Visit* (RUTC) and *The Grizzled Skipper at the Nuffield Theatre.*

Television includes *Midsomer Murders 'Dance With The Dead'* (ITV) and *Hidden* (BBC Wales).

Film includes *Footsteps* (Random Films).

Tara Wilkinson (Assistant Director)

Tara graduated from the post-graduate director's course at LAMDA in 2006.

Producing credits include *The Have Oak Trees in North Carolina* (Tristan Bates Theatre/Theatre503) and *The Final Shot* (Theatre503).

Assisting credits include *Terre Haute* (Assembly Rooms, Edinburgh Festival Fringe 2006, UK Tour and Trafalgar Studios 2007), *Three Days in April* (National Theatre Studio) and *The Accidental Lives of Memories* (The White Bear). She also assisted at The Royal Court as part of the theatre's 50th Anniversary.

Directing credits include *Flamingos* (Theatre Tent, Latitude Festival), *Unrequited* (Nabokov Shorts, Old Red Lion, London), an adaptation of Truman Capote's novella *Breakfast at Tiffany's*, LAMDA Duologue Showcase (Donmar Warehouse), *Ashes and Sand* (Linbury Studio, LAMDA), *The Memory of Water* and *Shakers* (both Alma Tavern, Bristol and Sweet on the Royal Mile, Edinburgh Festival Fringe).

bushfutures is a innovative education, training and development programme that allows emerging theatre professionals and members of the local community to access the expertise of Bush writers, directors, designers, technicians and actors. We are devoted to finding and supporting The Bush artists and audiences of tomorrow and the programme actively influences the future development of The Bush Theatre.

bushfutures **in schools**

bushfutures develops projects with schools, colleges and universities. The Bush is one of Britain's leading New Writing companies, and we want to share our talent and expertise with young people through tailor-made workshops which focus on writing, performance and the development of new work.

Halo Project – August 2008

Working with a Bush writer and director, emerging performers will discover and dramatise stories from the community here in Shepherds Bush. Come and discover the secret life of Shepherd's Bush here at The Bush Theatre.

Anthea Williams
bushfutures Co-Ordinator   bushfutures@bushtheatre.co.uk

Old Vic New Voices

Old Vic New Voices (OVNV) is a department of The Old Vic dedicated to supporting young and emerging talent, sourcing and developing new work for production on The Old Vic stage, and opening up the building to new and diverse audiences. For those embarking on a professional career in theatre, the New Voices Club offers actors, directors, producers and writers, aged 18-25, the opportunity to learn from industry professionals, receive support for projects they are passionate about through the New Voices Award, to experience New York theatre culture through the US/UK Exchange programme, and to network with like-minded peers. Entry is through The 24 Hour Plays: New Voices project, offering young practitioners the chance to take to The Old Vic stage and showcase their skills. Over the last two years, OVNV has worked with over 5000 young practitioners and facilitated the presentation of over 150 readings and development workshops – all key to nurturing the next generation of theatrical talent. For more information, see www.oldvictheatre.com/new

Kate Pakenham, Producer
Rachael Stevens, New Voices Manager
Steve Winter, Education and Community Manager

The Bush Theatre
'One of the most experienced prospectors of raw talent in Europe'

The Independent

The Bush Theatre is one of the most celebrated new writing theatres in the world. We have an international reputation for discovering, nurturing and producing the best new theatre writers from the widest range of backgrounds, and for presenting their work to the highest possible standards. We look for exciting new voices that tell contemporary stories with wit, style and passion and we champion work that is both provocative and entertaining.

With around 40,000 people enjoying our productions each year, The Bush has produced hundreds of ground-breaking premieres since its inception 35 years ago. The theatre produces up to eight productions of new plays a year, many of them Bush commissions, and hosts guest productions by leading companies and artists from all over the world.

The Bush is widely acclaimed as the seedbed for the best new playwrights, many of whom have gone on to become established names in the entertainment industry, including Steve Thompson, Jack Thorne, Amelia Bullmore, Dennis Kelly, Chloë Moss, David Eldridge, Stephen Poliakoff, Snoo Wilson, Terry Johnson, Kevin Elyot, Doug Lucie, Dusty Hughes, Sharman Macdonald, Billy Roche, Catherine Johnson, Philip Ridley, Richard Cameron, Jonathan Harvey, Conor McPherson, Joe Penhall, Helen Blakeman, Mark O'Rowe and Charlotte Jones. We also champion the introduction of new talent to the industry, whilst continuing to attract major acting and directing talents, including Richard Wilson, Nadim Sawalha, Bob Hoskins, Alan Rickman, Antony Sher, Stephen Rea, Frances Barber, Lindsay Duncan, Brian Cox, Kate Beckinsale, Patricia Hodge, Simon Callow, Alison Steadman, Jim Broadbent, Tim Roth, Jane Horrocks, Mike Leigh, Mike Figgis, Mike Newell, Victoria Wood and Julie Walters.

The Bush has won over one hundred awards, and developed an enviable reputation for touring its acclaimed productions nationally and internationally. Recent tours and transfers include the West End production of *Elling* (2007), the West End transfer and national tour of *Whipping it Up*, a national tour of *Mammals* (2006), an international tour of *After The End* (2005-6), *adrenalin... heart* representing the UK in the Tokyo International Arts Festival (2004), the West End transfer (2002) and national tour of *The Glee Club* (2004), a European tour of *Stitching* (2003) and Off-Broadway transfers of *Howie the Rookie* and *Resident Alien*. Film adaptations include *Beautiful Thing* and *Disco Pigs*.

The Bush Theatre provides a free script reading service, receiving over 1000 scripts through the post every year, and reading them all. This is one small part of a comprehensive Writers' Development Programme, which includes workshops, one-to-one dramaturgy, rehearsed readings, research bursaries, masterclasses, residencies and commissions. We have also launched a pilot scheme for an ambitious new education, training and professional development programme, **bush**futures, providing opportunities for different sectors of the community and professionals to access the expertise of Bush writers, directors, designers, technicians and actors, and to play an active role in influencing the future development of the theatre and its programme.

The Bush Theatre is extremely proud of its reputation for artistic excellence, its friendly atmosphere, and its undisputed role as a major force in shaping the future of British theatre.

Josie Rourke
Artistic Director

At The Bush Theatre

Artistic Director	**Josie Rourke**
General Manager	**Angela Bond**
Literary Manager	**Abigail Gonda**
Bushfutures Co-ordinator	**Anthea Williams**
Finance Manager	**Dave Smith**
Development Manager	**Sophie Hussey**
Development Officer	**Sara-Jane Westrop**
Chief Technician	**Tom White**
Resident Stage Manager	**Christabel Anderson**
Administrative Assistant	**Caroline Dyott**
Literary Assistant	**Jane Fallowfield**
Box Office Supervisor	**Ian Poole**
Box Office Assistants	**Sarah Ives, Fabiany de Castro Oliveira, Kirsty Cox**
Front of House Duty Managers	**Kellie Batchelor, Adrian Christopher, Alex Hern, Abigail Lumb, Glenn Mortimer, Kirstin Smith, Lois Tucker, Alicia Turrell**
Duty Technicians	**Jason Kirk, Mark Selby, Shelley Stace**
Associate Artists	**Tanya Burns, Chloe Emmerson, Richard Jordan, Paul Miller**
Pearson Writer in Residence	**Jack Thorne**
Press Representative	**Ewan Thomson & Giles Cooper at Borkowski**
Marketing	**Ben Jefferies at Spark Arts Marketing**

The Bush Theatre
Shepherds Bush Green
London W12 8QD

Box Office: 020 7610 4224
www.bushtheatre.co.uk

The Alternative Theatre Company Ltd. (The Bush Theatre)
is a Registered Charity number: 270080
Co. registration number 1221968
VAT no. 228 3168 73

supported by

Be There At The Beginning

Our work identifying and nurturing writers is only made possible through the generous support of our Patrons and other donors. Thank you to all those who have supported us during the last year.

If you are interested in finding out how to be involved, visit the 'Support Us' section of our website, email **development@bushtheatre.co.uk** or call 020 7602 3703.

Lone Star
Gianni Alen-Buckley
Catherine
& Pierre Lagrange
Princess of Darkness

Handful of Stars
Joe Hemani
Sarah Phelps

Glee Club
Anonymous
Bill & Judy Bollinger
Jim Broadbent
Clyde Cooper
Sophie Fauchier
Albert & Lynn Fuss
Piers & Melanie Gibson
Tanny Gordon
Adam Kenwright
Jacky Lambert
Curtis Brown Group Ltd
Richard & Elizabeth
Philipps
Alan Rickman
Paul & Jill Ruddock
John & Tita Shakeshaft
June Summerill
The Peter Wolff Theatre
Trust

Beautiful Thing
Anonymous
Mrs Oonagh Berry
John Bottrill
Seana Brennan
Alan Brodie
Kate Brooke
David Brooks
Clive Butler
Matthew Byam Shaw
Justin Coldwell
Jeremy Conway
Anna Donald
Alex Gammie
Vivien Goodwin
Sheila Hancock
David Hare
Lucy Heller
Francis & Mary-Lou Hussey
Bill Keeling

Jeremy & Britta Lloyd
Laurie Marsh
Ligeia Marsh
Michael McCoy
Tim McInnerny &
Annie Gosney
John Michie
David & Anita Miles
Mr & Mrs Philip Mould
John & Jacqui Pearson
Mr & Mrs A Radcliffe
Wendy Rawson
John Reynolds
Caroline Robinson
David Pugh
& Dafydd Rogers
Nadim Sawalha
Barry Serjent
Brian D Smith
Abigail Uden
Barrie & Roxanne Wilson

Rookies
Anonymous
Neil Adleman
Tony Allday
Ross Anderson
Pauline Asper
Mr and Mrs Badrichani
Tanya Burns
& Sally Crabb
Constance Byam Shaw
Geraldine Caufield
Nigel Clark
Alan Davidson
Joy Dean
Nina Drucker
Miranda Greig
Sian Hansen
Mr G Hopkinson
Joyce Hytner, ACT IV
Robert Israel
for Gordon & Co.
Peter James
Hardeep Kalsi
Casarotto Ramsay &
Associates Ltd
Robin Kermode
Ray Miles
Mr & Mrs Malcolm Ogden
Julian & Amanda

Platt Radfin
Clare Rich
Mark Roberts
David Robinson
Councillor Minnie Scott
Russell
Martin Shenfield
John Trotter
Loveday Waymouth
Clare Williams
Alison Winter

Platinum Corporate members
Anonymous

Silver
The Agency (London) Ltd
Peters, Fraser & Dunlop

Bronze
Act Productions Ltd
Artists Rights Group
Hat Trick Productions
Orion Management

Trust and foundation supporters
The John S Cohen
Foundation
The Earls Court and
Olympia Charitable Trust
The Ernest Cook Trust
Garfield Weston
Foundation
The Girdlers' Company
Charitable Trust
The John Thaw
Foundation
The Kobler Trust
The Martin Bowley
Charitable Trust
The Mercers' Company
The Royal Victoria Hall
Charitable Trust
The Thistle Trust
The Vandervell
Foundation
The Harold Hyam Wingate
Foundation

Artefacts

For my Mum

Characters

Kelly
Susan
Ibrahim
Faiza
Raya

(/) *means the next speech begins at that point.*

(–) *means the next line interrupts.*

(. . .) *at the end of a speech means it trails off. On its own, it indicates a pressure, expectation or desire to speak.*

A speech with no written dialogue indicates a character deliberately remaining silent.

Blank space between speeches in the dialogue indicates time drifting on with slightly less happening for a moment.

Thanks to Hassan Abdulrazzak and Abdul Karim Kasid for the Arabic translations; Chris Campbell, Ramin Gray, Ben Jancovic, Clare Lizzimore, Kate Packenham, Rachael Stevens, Lyndsey Turner, Rachael Wagstaff, Josie Rouke, the Bush Theatre, the Royal Court Theatre, Old Vic New Voices, Nabokov Theatre, and to all the actors who helped develop the play.

And particularly Emma Brunjes and James Grieve, without whom this play would never have been written.

Part One

Scene One

Kelly *stands with her bag.*

Kelly I just wanted one of those Saturdays, one of those good rainy Saturday afternoons when you lie back, watch a film, call your mates, text a boy, yeah? But this afternoon had just been weird cos my phone wasn't ringing, no one had plans, Mum's stressed downstairs with work and I'm kind of trapped in my room cos it's raining, I've homework to do which I know I'm not gonna and there's nothing on TV but football and antiques. So all in all it's kind of depressing?

He's downstairs. Saw his coat.

And yeah, so I was walking in circles and I moved my furniture around and tried on different clothes in different combinations and I know what it's all about, it's cos of what I want to look like tomorrow cos *tomorrow*'s when I thought we were going to meet.

Susan *enters.*

Susan I heard you come in.

Kelly Did you. Well done.

Susan Love, he's been waiting –

Kelly Not my fault.

Susan – and he has to go soon, he's only –

Kelly Give me a minute.

Susan . . .

Susan *goes.*

Kelly She only told me yesterday. It's Friday night, I'd got back from school and I'm going straight down the pub with my mate Sarah and this bunch of lads from St Nics – some of them are quite fit – and I was late but she stops me on the way out and says Kelly we have to talk. She always picks moments like that to stop me moments when it's going to be a problem. What? What is it? And she says it's your dad. He's coming round on Sunday.

Er. I thought he didn't want to see us?

He walked out on you, you hate him, you don't know where he is, he's probably dead. Well he's not, Kelly. He's coming for lunch. On Sunday. Turns out she had stayed in contact with him after all, but he lived abroad and hadn't wanted to see me until now. Why? She didn't know. Where has he been then?

Get this.

Iraq.

Jesus.

Baghdad.

What, does he work for a charity or . . .

No.

He's from Iraq.

So I'm half Iraqi.

Shit man.

I said I had to go, went to the pub and got my pint and Sarah was asking me had someone died cos I wasn't saying anything, which for me is unusual. But I was thinking – who is he? Does he have a family? Have I got a brother or a sister? Has he got a big tongue? Cos all my family have got small tongues but mine is massive, look . . .

She sticks her tongue out.

And Mum's family are all good looking, all quite fit, but I'm not? So he's probably –

Ibrahim *enters.*

Ibrahim   Kelly.

Kelly Ugly.

Oh.

Hi.

Dad.

Ibrahim I'm Ibrahim.

Will they hug? They move a little closer.

He puts out his hand.

She shakes it.

I'm pleased to meet you at last.

Kelly Yeah.

Sorry.

Sorry.

Ibrahim *smiles slightly.*

Ibrahim Would you like a moment?

Kelly Yeah I would actually, thanks.

Thinking all these questions. Who would he be? Who would he expect me to be?

Actually no. Fuck off. He left, twat. I've got nothing I need to prove. If I *choose* to see him then that's y'know, that's different. That's my choice. I grant him that. I grant him an audience. You may see me now, Father.

I'll look like I look, I'll wear what I want.

Ibrahim Where do we start?

Kelly Don't know. Favourite colour?

Ibrahim Am I . . . what you expected?

Kelly Mum only told me you existed yesterday.

Ibrahim Yes.

Kelly   So no.

You're not what I expected.

Ibrahim   Who did you imagine I might be?

Kelly   A secret agent.

Ibrahim   A –

Kelly   Yeah, I thought you were like James Bond or whatever and that if anyone knew that I was your daughter that would put me in danger. So even though it broke your heart you pretended I didn't exist, to protect me.

Cos when I was little I didn't understand why you weren't there.

Ibrahim   I'm sorry.

Kelly   Cos you could have written, couldn't you?

Mum asked, do I want to get him a present or something? Do I? No. Like what? He's come from Iraq. I could probably give him a Mars bar and he'd be amazed. But no. Yeah. Maybe I should.

Ibrahim   Actually I did / write . . .

Kelly   Something to help him get to know me. So I looked through my room trying to find something that would sum me up and then I got it and this is brilliant, cos in the back of my cupboard, there's this old maths exercise book, from when I was thirteen. Now there's not much maths cos that's shit and I can't do it but in the back are all these scribblins and hearts, stuff like 'Paul Franklin is a penis' and 'Boredom equals Death', whatever that is. And I reckon it would give him a good idea of who I am, what I'm like. So I'm going to give him that.

Ibrahim   I did write, but your mother –

Kelly   What?

Ibrahim   She didn't pass the letters on.

Kelly   Why not?

Ibrahim   She didn't want you to know about me. / Not at –

Kelly   Why not? Are you a murderer?

Ibrahim   No.

Kelly   You haven't killed anyone?

Ibrahim   No.

Kelly   I thought you was from Iraq?

Ibrahim   Yes, but –

Kelly   Weren't you in the war?

Ibrahim   I didn't fight.

Kelly   Why not? Scared?

Ibrahim   She didn't pass on the letters –

Kelly   I'd be scared.

Ibrahim   – because maybe she thought you might go looking for me.

Kelly   What? In –

Ibrahim   Yes.

Kelly   I'm not going there.

Ibrahim   You –

Kelly   I'll get my head cut off.

Won't I?

Ibrahim   I don't know.

Kelly   On video.

Ibrahim   I suppose / that's possible.

Kelly   Probably would do. Got a big mouth see? Just say what I think. Can't shut up.

Ibrahim   Perhaps you get that from me.

Kelly   Nah, my uncle.

Ibrahim   Do you think we look alike?

Kelly   You and my uncle?

Ibrahim   You and me.

Kelly   Um . . . No.

Ibrahim   You're passionate.

Kelly   I'm English.

Ibrahim   You are half Iraqi. You can have an Iraqi passport now.

Kelly   That's not much use

Ibrahim   Would you prefer it if I had been an American?

Kelly   No.

Well, yeah. That would be better though, wouldn't it? Cos an American passport's worth loads. I could go there and work and stuff. But I told you I'm not going to go to Iraq, am I?

Susan *enters.*

Susan   You can come downstairs if you want.

Kelly   No thanks.

Susan   When do you want the taxi for? I'll call now.

Ibrahim   Oh . . . ten minutes.

Kelly   Ten minutes?

Ibrahim   Thank you.

Susan   Right.

Kelly   This afternoon when I was bored I looked in the mirror cos, apparently, I'm half Iraqi.

Susan *hesitates.*

Susan   Are you sure you're both / all right?

Kelly   But which bits?

Susan   Up here?

Kelly Hips. / Hands.

Ibrahim Kelly?

Kelly I've got English legs. / Iraqi breasts.

Ibrahim I wish we could've / met earlier.

Kelly But my stomach is slightly potted.

Ibrahim Kelly?

Susan I'll leave you to it.

Susan *goes.*

Kelly I have a little pot belly. Maybe this is the point they mix. The two countries. Where my genes got confused. This belly is not Iraqi or English. It's Engraqi. Iringlish. I like my belly. Yeah.

She looks at **Ibrahim**. *He is about to speak.*

Yeah, and then I got bored of looking naked in the mirror so I put some clothes on but they seem fake? And my room felt small. Claustrophobic? So I went out shopping. Even though it was raining. Am I what you expected?

Ibrahim I tried not to expect anything.

Kelly But you did.

Ibrahim I imagined you might look like Kate Winslet.

Kelly This isn't going very well, is it?

Ibrahim I don't know.

Kelly Bit of a fucking disappointment for you.

Ibrahim No.

Kelly If you were after –

Ibrahim You are better than / Kate Winslet.

Kelly What do you want?

Ibrahim You are you.

Kelly   Why are you here? Now. What do you *want*?

Ibrahim   That we meet.

Kelly   Just that.

Ibrahim   Yes.

Kelly   You don't want money?

Ibrahim

Kelly

Ibrahim   I run the National Museum of Iraq. In Baghdad. A number of our artefacts were stolen. During the war. I was invited to come and give a lecture at the British Museum about the current state of our collection. That is where I have been today.

Kelly   So I'm not actually why you came at all.

Ibrahim   It is expensive to fly here. I will probably never come back to Britain. So I thought it best we meet.

Kelly

Ibrahim   And I wanted to give you something.

Kelly   What?

Yeah. I brought a present for you too.

Kelly *gives him her maths book.*

There.

Ibrahim   What is . . . ?

Kelly   It's my maths exercise book, from when I was thirteen.

But I'm not good at maths, so I wrote loads of other stuff in it, like things about . . .

Ibrahim (*reading*)   'Paul Franklin is a penis.'

Kelly   Yeah, but other stuff. I thought you might find out who I really am.

Ibrahim   Thank you.

Thank you.

Ibrahim *reads the book.*

Kelly I hate shopping on my own. I feel like such a Kelly-no-mates so I've given up but I didn't want to go home. It's better out. So I'm having a Coke, reading the *Heat* and my phone rings. It's Mum. Jesus. I'm reading about Cameron Diaz. I put it on silent, I think she's mental, there's this thing about the top ten fat legs. Charlotte Church is at three. They should have Fern Britton in that. She's massive. Put another sugar in my Coke. There's a picture of this girl with her tits out. My legs feel fat now. Look at people opposite me, they look depressed. Then my phone's ringing again. Mum. Jesus. Leave me alone. It's seven o'clock. I leave. Walk. Hate London. Don't care where I go. What did you get me?

He smiles.

Ibrahim I brought you something very valuable.

He lifts up his bag. Starts to unpack the box.

Kelly But it's raining. And this guy with a megaphone is shouting at me in the street. He says, don't be sinner be a winner. Yeah, OK – I'm not. He says, I'm fat, I'm evil, repent repent yeah yeah, shouldn't let people like that out, I walk on. I want to get lost. But I can't. I've lived here all my life. I know the streets too well.

Ibrahim *takes out a box.*

Puts it on the table.

Unpack it.

But be very careful.

Kelly *starts to unpack it.*

Kelly My phone's vibrating again, obviously it's Mum, and now I'm just walking in the rain with nothing to do so I answer. What? You have to come home cos your dad has to get an earlier plane than he thought, so he's come round tonight instead and he's only got a couple of hours now so come back.

And I'm about to say I'm busy but I know I'm not. There's no way out of this so back I go.

Kelly *lifts out what's inside. A very old Mesopotamian pot. She looks at it.*

Did you get this in Debenhams or something?

Ibrahim   It's one of the most ancient vases in the world.

Kelly   Is it worth something then?

I'm not saying I'm going to sell it.

Ibrahim   It's priceless.

Kelly   So it is, or . . .

Ibrahim   It's worth more than money.

Kelly   Why have you got it?

Ibrahim   I told you. I run the museum.

Kelly   You stole it.

Ibrahim   I have signed a form in Baghdad to say that it is on loan to the British Museum. I have then signed a form earlier today in London that confirms the change of plan and that this vase will stay in Baghdad. Therefore, officially it is in two places at once.

Kelly   You stole it / then.

Ibrahim   If anyone looks, it will not be found. It belongs to Iraq. I just want you to look after it while things are still . . .

Kelly   Sounds illegal.

Ibrahim   It's what I want.

As your father.

Kelly   Cancel your flight.

That's what I want.

As your daughter.

Ibrahim   Maybe you do not understand.

Kelly   Spend some time / with me.

Ibrahim   This vase is Iraq, before Iraq it was Assyria, Mesopotamia. It is wisdom, it is beauty, its adornment is entirely unnecessary, and that makes it invaluable when your country is disappearing. We are fighting so that one day we will be able to appreciate this vase in peace.

Kelly   Why did you leave us?

Ibrahim   If you have this. You have me.

Kelly   Before I was born.

Ibrahim   . . .

Kelly

Ibrahim   My family was being threatened.

Kelly   We were your family.

Ibrahim   Then it was not long before / the Americans –

Kelly   We needed you.

Ibrahim   This is Britain. This is safe.

Kelly   When I was fourteen I got beaten up by this gang from St Anthony's. They kicked me to the ground. I still got a scar. I lost a tooth. I wanted my dad to go round and sort them out. But he wasn't here.

Ibrahim   I'm here now.

Kelly   And you've got four minutes left. So what next?

She puts down the pot.

I don't want it. What if we're broken in?

Ibrahim   No one knows it is here.

That is the beauty of this arrangement.

Kelly   Arrangement?

Ibrahim   This is the best way. I am killing two birds with one stone. Yes?

Kelly   What?

Ibrahim   Sorry. Not . . . killing two birds.

Kelly   Nice, Dad, nice.

Ibrahim   It will be a link between us. Maybe one day you will come and visit me. Visit your country.

Kelly   I don't know anything about it.

Ibrahim   Find out.

Kelly   I've got things to do too. Revision.

Ibrahim   Ask me questions now. Let's get to know each other.

Kelly   You have to leave to get your plane. Unless you get one tomorrow. If you get one tomorrow I'll pay.

Ibrahim   It's not the money. They have brought the flight forward. I didn't know we would have such a short time. But Kelly –

Kelly   Three and a / half minutes.

Ibrahim   Kelly, there must be things you want to know.

Kelly   Loads.

Ibrahim   Pick one for now.

Kelly   Have I got a brother or a sister?

Ibrahim   Yes. A sister.

Kelly   What's her name?

Ibrahim   Raya.

Kelly   How old is she?

Ibrahim   Thirteen.

Do you want to see a picture?

Ibrahim *gives* **Kelly** *a small picture of* **Raya**.

She's very pretty, isn't she?

Kelly *looks at it.*

Kelly   Didn't you ever want a photo of me?

She hands back the picture.

Didn't you miss me?

Ibrahim   Sometimes.

Kelly   Every day?

Ibrahim   No.

Kelly   I thought about you every day.

Ibrahim   Kelly. You are happy.

Here.

Susan *enters.*

Ibrahim   You didn't need me.

Maybe you were better off with just your mum.

Kelly   You don't get it? Do you?

Susan   The taxi's outside.

Ibrahim   Thank you.

Kelly   Yeah. Good to meet you then, stay in touch, bye.

She picks up the pot. Looks at it. She is crying. **Susan** *exchanges a look with* **Ibrahim** *and then goes.*

Ibrahim   Your mum has my address.

We will write but I have to –

Kelly   You want to get out of here as soon as you can, don't you?

Ibrahim   I don't think it's good to just cry.

Kelly *turns back. Looks directly at him.*

Kelly   I might smash the pot if you go.

Ibrahim   That would be up to you.

I have to trust that you won't, but –

Kelly   If you just leave now, I will I'll drop it.

Ibrahim   Don't be stupid.

Kelly

Ibrahim *goes to* **Kelly** *to kiss her goodbye. She moves away.*

Ibrahim   You will come to visit me one day, yes?

Kelly   I'm serious.

Ibrahim   I have to go.

Kelly   I will.

Ibrahim   Goodbye.

Kelly   Don't.

He turns.

Walks away.

She drops the vase on the floor.

It smashes into three pieces.

He looks at it.

They both stare at the floor.

Ibrahim

Kelly

He leaves.

Scene Two

Faiza *is sitting by the table, reading a story to* **Raya** *in Arabic.*

Faiza   *Kan ya makan. Kan honak ʿazef mizmar, ʾkadama ella ʾkarya tamlaʾoha alfeeran. Kall leʾahloha annaaʾastaʾteeʾoo en atrooda alfeeran mogabel alef ʾkotta thahabiya. Fa-wafakoo wa ʾkaloo lahoo: naʾateek kool shii etha abʾadta alfeeran ʿannaa. Andatha nafakha al-azeefo fee mezmarehee fa-tabaʾhoo gameeoo alfeeran. Wa ibtaʾada biha ʿan alkarya. Ahtafal ahloo alkarya wa saharoo teelka al-lella farheen.* [Once there was a piper. He came to a village which had many rats and he said, I can take them all away for one thousand gold pieces. The people of the village said, yes we will give you anything to take the rats away. So the piper played his pipe and the rats all followed him and were taken away from the village. The people of the village celebrated that the rats had gone. They celebrated all night.]

Mara esbooʾ, aada azeef almezmar leeistilam al-alfoo ʾkottaa thahabeyia. Lakeen sookan alʾkarya lem yedfʾaoo lahoo leʾannahoom la yemleekoon shii wa-la ahad yazoor ʾkaryatahoom. Lekkad akalat alfeeran kool ma yemleekoon min taʾam. Kanoo fookaraa wa la yaʾareefoon keef yedfaʾoon almableegh ella azeef almezmar. Thaar azeef almezmar lee-nafsah. Fa-nafakha fee mezmarh thanyia. Leem taʾatba-ʾhoo hathehee almara alfeeran bel al-atfaal. Kool atfaal alkarya. Ka-dahoom al-ʿazeef wa abta-ʿadda bihim an alkarya fa-akhtafoo ella alabbad. Ma-ʿadda tefaal wahed lem yesta-ʿateeʾ al-eltahaaq bihim lemoshkila fee reglho fa-ʿaad ella alkarya le-yokhbir ahlaha. [A week later the piper came back and asked for his thousand gold pieces. But the people of the village could not pay the money. They had nothing, because the rats had eaten all their food, and no one had been coming to the village. The people were too poor and they had not thought of how they would pay the piper. So the piper took his revenge. And he played the pipe and all the children of the village came out and followed him. The piper took all the children from the village away for ever. Except for one boy, who could not keep up as he had a bad leg. He came back to the village and told them.]

Len taroon atfalakom thaanya. [You will never see your children again.]

Len taroon atfalakom thaanya. [You will never see your children again.]

Scene Three

Kelly *sits at the table with* **Susan**. *They both have cups of tea.*

The pieces of the vase and a pile of old letters are on the table.

Susan   I was on the sofa watching television. *Going for Gold.* That was on. He comes in and switches it off. Says he's leaving. He's quitting his degree, and going back home to start a new job at the museum. I thought it was a joke, but he spent an hour packing his stuff and then walked out. I was left on the couch, with you, not yet born.

He got scared, Kelly. Lots of men do.

The letters are because he felt guilty.

Come on. Look at me, sweetheart.

You've been better off without them.

Sweetheart.

We're still all right, aren't we?

Kelly   You never loved him then?

Susan   I –

Kelly   I was a mistake.

Susan   No.

Kelly   I mean you didn't want me . . . with him.

Susan   No. I suppose I didn't want you with him. I wanted you with someone who would have stayed.

Kelly   Then I wouldn't be me.

Susan

Kelly   Is this all of them?

Susan   Yes.

Kelly   I'm sixteen? Isn't it up to me to know who he is, whether I want to see him or not?

Susan   I tried to protect you.

Kelly   Anything else you're not telling me?

Susan   No.

Kelly   Anything else you're *protecting* me from?

Susan   I brought you tea.

Kelly   How do I know you're telling the truth?

Susan   It's getting cold, sweetheart.

Kelly   I don't give a shit about the fucking tea, yeah?

Susan

Kelly *looks at the letters.*

Ibrahim   Thank you so much for spending the time to meet me last night. It was very kind of you, and it all made so much more clear for me. I find it difficult to write in English.

Susan   It has been fun getting to know you. It is very boring at home. I still think of the fountain, that first week. Do you remember?

Ibrahim   We drank two bottles of whisky.

Susan   I miss you.

Ibrahim   Each.

Susan   You called me *habib-tea.*

Ibrahim   I carried you over my shoulder.

Susan   This feels serious, doesn't it?

Ibrahim   Happy birthday.

Susan   I don't think my mother had met anyone from Iraq before.

Ibrahim   Happy birthday, my princess.

Susan   Princess?

Ibrahim   I did not intend to fall in love. But it is perfect. You are perfect.

Susan   I can't stop thinking about your body.

Ibrahim   But –

Susan   Thank you for your understanding while I have been away.

Ibrahim   What will happen when I finish my degree?

Susan   I miss your beard.

Ibrahim   Thank you for the photographs.

Susan   I know it is not what you want.

Ibrahim

Susan   And you must tell me the truth. What do you think? I will come back and we can stay together. Are you happy?

Ibrahim

Susan   You must be honest.

Ibrahim   This is a blessing. This is a wonderful thing. I look forward to seeing you.

Susan   I love you.

Ibrahim   This is a beginning.

Susan   Ibrahim, I don't know if this is even the right address.

Ibrahim

Susan   I am just writing to your family home in the hope that it will reach you. I am obviously devastated, but I don't want anything from you. I will not need you to raise our daughter. I have called her Kelly, and I will send you a copy of my Christmas letter each year so you know how she is. Apart from this I will not write again.

Ibrahim   My dear Kelly, on your fifth birthday, I hope you like this picture of a clown. I think it is funny. I hope you have had a lovely day. I think you start school this year. Work hard, because from what I understand, you are very clever indeed.

I love you very much, Kelly. Lots of my love, Daddy.

Susan   Dear Ibrahim,

I have no intention of passing your card on to our daughter. It has been five years. You have made it quite clear that you do not want to be part of her life. Have you thought how much more damage a single message like this every year will do? As Kelly grows up she will know that you *can* contact her, that you *could* visit, but that you are choosing not to. I am simply going to tell her that I don't know where you are. She deserves better.

Kelly   Mum.

Thanks for the tea.

Susan   Right.

Kelly   Sorry.

Susan   Yes.

Susan *goes.*

Ibrahim   Dear Kelly, on your sixth birthday. Your mother will not pass these letters on, but I will keep writing. I hear you have not been very happy at school this year, and that some of the other children have been nasty to you. Don't let them worry you. They are just jealous of how beautiful and intelligent you are. I hope you are having a lovely day. I am, of course, sorry I will not be there.

Lots of love to my little Kelly. Daddy.

Kelly   Sorry I broke your pot.

Can you change your mind and come back now, please?

Ibrahim

Kelly   I would like to write to my sister.

Does she speak English?

Ibrahim *goes.*

Daddy?

It's Kelly.

Your

Your little Kelly.

Part Two

Scene One

Kelly *is sitting at a table, wearing her travelling clothes.*

Kelly   So. Get me. I'm the shit. I've done my homework. And now I know all about it. They reckon this is Eden. Where we come from cos this is the cradle of civilisation, home to the world's first proper society the Sumerians who had the hanging gardens of Babylon and then it's the Mongols which is where that comes from you know 'urrgh mongoloid', and then at the end of the nineteenth century it becomes part of the Ottoman Empire. The Ottoman Empire had control over the land that's now Iraq, which at this point was these three kingdoms with three cities, Mosul in the north, Baghdad in the middle and Basra in the bottom, and that went on all the way up until the First World War. And it was actually officials of the Ottoman Empire, in the early part of the twentieth century, that first used the word Iraq, which either comes from a Sumerian city called Uruk, or is derived from the Aramaic for 'the land along the banks of the rivers', to describe these three areas, but at this point it was *not*. Right? *Not* a separate country or thought of in that way. Oh no. Got all this off Wikipedia. Learnt it.

Faiza *enters*

Kelly   Hi.

That smells amazing.

Faiza *hands Arabic coffee to* **Kelly**.

Kelly   Thank you.

Faiza *picks up an Arabic–English dictionary.*

Kelly *drinks the coffee.*

Hmmm.

She gives a thumbs up sign.

Good.

Faiza *sits down.*

A slightly awkward moment.

Kelly   Then at the beginning of the First World War, Britain went into the southern territory and occupied Basra. They then took Baghdad and Mosul and over the next twenty years, with a lot of politics and the United Nations and stuff in 1932, Britain created Iraq. We made it up.

No one at home knows that but it's so important. We're all so ignorant. We're all so *lazy*.

I'm also learning Arabic. Got a CD out from the library. Went up to the woman – 'Um, excuse me do you have a course in Arabic?' She looked well impressed. Got it on my iPod. Yeah? So –

Faiza   *Teshbaheen Raya.* [You look like Raya.]

Kelly *looks at her. Clueless.*

Faiza *goes and looks up words in her dictionary.*

Kelly   But Arabic's really difficult?

Faiza   You.

Kelly   So I used to put on Kanye West instead. Me?

Faiza   Hot?

Kelly   Hot?

Faiza   No? *Ha-ret-lech?* [Hot?] Yes?

Kelly   Oh yes.

Faiza   *Mistahya?* [You're nervous?]

Kelly   Um. *Shokran.* [Thank you.]

Faiza   Arabic?

Kelly Yeah. A bit.

Faiza *Tamam.* [Good.]

Kelly I . . .hot. *Ha-ret-lech.* [Hot.]Um. Dirty. Um. Dirty.

Uuergh. Dirty.

Faiza *Treedeen teghisleen?* [Do you want a bath? To wash?]

Kelly ?

Faiza *looks up a word in the dictionary.*

Faiza Er. You.

Wash?

Kelly No.

I'm OK.

OK?

Faiza OK.

She looks up words.

I . . . will hot . . .

I will hot . . .

Water.

I will hot water.

She leaves.

Kelly I kept writing to Dad but he didn't reply. So I just get on with my life, go on holiday to France, fall off a wall, nearly get pregnant, do my A levels and everyone's amazed but I do all right. Got my place in Sheffield and now I got a long summer before I go. Then Mum gets a call. He wants me to visit. I'm like no. I'm busy. Fuck off please. But then we end up talking and it's really important actually and I'm not doing anything so I don't have an excuse, except obviously all the bombs and stuff, but somehow it gets sorted and a week later I go on a three-day safety course that Mum said she'd pay for where it's me and all these journalists with moustaches giving me weird looks and that's just the women.

Faiza *comes in, holding a towel. She gives it to* **Kelly**.

Faiza   Wash.

Kelly   *Shokran.* [Thank you.] Maybe later?

Faiza   No wash?

Kelly   *Shokran.* [Thank you]

Faiza   *Hamatlech al-mayee.* [I've heated the water.]

Kelly   Sorry . . . I don't –

Faiza   *Mo haramat.* [I don't want to waste it.]

Kelly   ?

Faiza *leaves with the towel.*

Kelly   Yeah, then we sort out the visa and the passport and check it's all OK and make arrangements and before I know it I've flown over – London to Amman, Amman to Baghdad, and I'm in a car with security that I've paid for to get me from the airport to this house, and I'm looking out the window and it's weird, cos I've got armour and security and I'm travelling through these streets like I'm going to be shot any moment but outside there's people talking and mums with pushchairs, and people shopping and stuff. You know. There's traffic jams and traffic lights. It's amazing. It's normal. The driver points out places of interest. Old palaces and big houses and stuff. He keeps on saying 'before'. 'Before' there used to be a market here. 'Before' kids used to play football, there was not this traffic 'before'. There's a bit of stone by the side of the road where there must have been a statue. I want to ask if it was of Saddam Hussein. But get this . . . I kept my mouth shut. Oh yeah. Mouth. Shut.

Faiza *comes and sits opposite* **Kelly**. *They smile.*

Kelly   He says I'm very young. The driver. He asks how old I am. I tell him. Eighteen. He says 'beautiful' twice. Beautiful.

Then he says, am I on a gap year? In a way. I'm visiting family. I tell him my dad's Iraqi. I'm Iraqi. And the driver smiles and goes, have I been here before?

No.

Then he says, 'You are coming home, yes? Welcome home.'

Ibrahim *enters.*

Ibrahim   *Rah-yentather-knee hell lella.* [He'll be waiting for me tonight.]

Faiza   *Sh'ged?* [How long?]

Ibrahim   *Sa'aa.* [An hour.]

Faiza   *Tamam.* [Good.]

Kelly   It's amazing.

To be here.

Baghdad.

It's properly life-changing.

Ibrahim   Good.

Kelly   Was it all right?

Ibrahim   Yes.

Ibrahim *sits.* **Kelly** *does the same.*

Ibrahim   You look older.

Kelly   How?

Ibrahim   You have grown up.

Kelly   Thanks.

Ibrahim   You look like a woman now.

Kelly   So do you.

Ibrahim

Kelly   Look older, I mean.

Got more grey hair. You can get stuff for that.

Ibrahim

Kelly   I don't normally like coffee. But this is / different . . .

Ibrahim   Arabic coffee.

Kelly   It's sweet.

Ibrahim   Yes.

Kelly   I'll get some to take home. Mum likes coffee and I'm always like, no, I'll have tea, but if I bring this back . . .

Ibrahim   We'll have something to eat in a minute.

Kelly   OK.

I'm all right, thanks. Had something on the plane.

No one at home thought I'd actually do it? First they thought I was joking they were like no way you can't go there you're not allowed, they thought I'd probably wuss out in the end or not be bothered but they were wrong.

I'll send them a postcard.

I love your house.

Ibrahim   Good.

Kelly   It's really normal.

Ibrahim

Kelly   I mean, I thought I'd be sat here thinking a bomb was gonna come through the window or whatever. That any moment the door would burst open and troops would come in but it's not like that is it? From what you see on the TV, you think it's really bad all the time.

Kelly   Like every minute someone's firing a gun at you.

Faiza   Kelly.

Arabic.

Ibrahim Arabic?

Kelly Yeah.

Ibrahim Good.

Kelly I learnt it off a tape so I'm / a bit shit −

Ibrahim Say something in Arabic.

Faiza *leaves.*

Kelly What?

Ibrahim I would like to hear you.

Kelly Nah, I can't really − what?

Ibrahim Whatever you've learnt.

Kelly *Hathehee alsayarra kathera.* [This car is dirty.]

Ibrahim ?

Kelly Is that right? *Hathehee alsayarra kathera.* [This car is dirty.]

Ibrahim You are saying your car is dirty?

Kelly Yeah.

Ibrahim Why did you learn that?

Kelly It was on the tape.

Ibrahim That is classical Arabic.

Kelly Is it not right?

Ibrahim It is a different dialect in Iraq.

Kelly Don't I get points for trying?

No?

Are you going to do it tonight?

Ibrahim I wanted to pick you up today from the airport, but it sounds like you had it all planned −

Kelly Yeah, I got all this security.

Ibrahim   Good.

Kelly   I don't think I needed it.

Ibrahim   It is better you did. Anything can happen.

Kelly   Yeah.

Ibrahim   And you stand out.

Kelly   I tried to dress right.

Ibrahim   It is not your clothes.

Not just your clothes.

Faiza *enters with some food.*

Ibrahim   *Shokran.* [Thank you.]

Faiza *puts it down and sits with them. Offers some to* **Kelly**.

Ibrahim   *Matreed takol.* [She says she does not want to eat.]

Faiza   *Sawayena-ha alla-modha.* [We made this for her.]

Ibrahim   *Heyia hechi.* [This is what she is like.]

Faiza   *Mo mosh-killa itha matreed takool hesa.* [It is not important. If she doesn't want to eat now.]

Ibrahim   *Asfa ya habib-tea.* [I'm sorry, sweetheart.]

Faiza   *Addnaa homoom akbar.* [We have more important things to worry about.]

Ibrahim   Are you sure you don't want to eat something?

Kelly   I don't eat meat.

Ibrahim   This is not meat.

Kelly   Oh. It looks like it.

Ibrahim   You told us you were vegetarian. So this is for you.

Kelly   Thanks.

Ibrahim   Faiza made it for you.

Kelly   Oh. Thanks.

She takes a bit. They eat.

Faiza   *Teshba-hek.* [She looks like you.]

Ibrahim   *La'.* [No.]

Faiza   *Titmana lo chanet ma teshbahek?* [You wish she didn't?]

Ibrahim   *Inti thaycha min-ha?* [You don't mind her staying?]

Faiza   *La'.* [No.]

Ibrahim   *Ayenha tal'aa.* [She's rude.]

Faiza   *Ted haweel.* [At least she is trying.]

Ibrahim   *Ma-tesma' al kalam.* [She doesn't listen.]

Faiza   *Methlak.* [So she *is* like you.]

Kelly   You're going out tonight then?

Ibrahim   Yes. I do not want to waste time now that you are here.

Kelly   How old is she now?

Ibrahim   Fifteen.

Kelly   And do you know if she's –

Ibrahim   No. We don't know anything. How is your mother?

Kelly   What?

Ibrahim   Your mother.

Kelly   Oh. Yeah. Normal.

Ibrahim   I thought she might try to stop you coming.

Kelly   No.

Ibrahim   But you said she was happy.

Kelly   She was fine.

Ibrahim   Yes.

Kelly   Sort of.

Ibrahim   ?

Kelly   I mean she hid my passport. Called the British
Embassy. Went eppy. Cried loads. All that. Threw a biro at me.
Locked me in the house.

Ibrahim   You told me she agreed.

Kelly   Yeah, she did, in the end.

She couldn't stop me really.

Ibrahim   I would not have let you come. You said that she
agreed.

Kelly   Exactly.

Ibrahim   It is up to her. You are her daughter.

Kelly   And yours.

Yours too.

And you said this was important.

Ibrahim   Yes.

Yes. It is important.

Kelly   So do you want to know what I've been doing?

Ibrahim   Did you bring it?

Kelly   Yeah.

Ibrahim   . . .

Kelly   I was just wanting to say that I'm sorry.

When I wrote.

Ibrahim   Can I see it?

Kelly *starts to unpack the pot.*

Kelly   Did you get them?

Ibrahim   What?

Kelly   My letters?

Ibrahim   Yes.

Kelly   Right, cos you didn't reply.

So I wasn't sure.

Ibrahim   Did you wrap the pieces separately?

Kelly   Did you even read them?

Ibrahim   It has to be complete.

Kelly *stops unwrapping. Looks at him.*

Ibrahim   No. I didn't.

Kelly   But you've still got them?

Ibrahim   Yes.

Kelly   I'll have them back then.

Ibrahim   Whatever you want.

Kelly   If you're not interested.

Ibrahim   I was worried you would take it to someone to fix it.

Kelly   Wouldn't that be better?

Ibrahim   No, you would need an expert.

Kelly   No, I didn't take it to anyone.

Ibrahim   Good.

She gets out the vase. It is crudely glued together.

She puts it on the table.

Kelly   I did it myself.

He picks it up.

Ibrahim   What with?

Kelly   Superglue.

Faiza   *Shinnoo?* [What?]

Ibrahim   *Shoofie!* [Look at it!]

D-shoofie! [Look at it!]

Kelly   I was trying to help.

Ibrahim   I told you this was priceless.

Kelly   Yeah.

Ibrahim   Thousands of years old.

Kelly   All right, I know it was a bit stupid, probably wasn't the best way to do it, but I was only sixteen so . . .

Ibrahim   It is a mess.

Kelly   Everyone's stupid when they're sixteen, yeah? Bet even you were stupid then. It's still worth something though, right?

Ibrahim   You should have just given me the pieces.

Why didn't you tell me you had done this?

Kelly   I thought it might be good.

Ibrahim   Why wait till now?

Kelly   I thought you might like it.

Ibrahim   *Shoofie.* [Look.]

Yemkin may reedha. [He may not want it.]

Faiza   *Lazem it-hawill.* [You have to try.]

Kelly   I was trying / to do the right thing.

Ibrahim   *Merah enhassel al kafi.* [He will not give us enough.]

Faiza   *Shin-sawi? Nith-terr nistelef.* [What else can we do? If we don't get enough we will have to borrow the money.]

Ibrahim   *Min-men?* [Who from?]

Kelly   But it's really / not about me, is it?

Fazia   *In-hawill.* [We've got to try.]

Ibrahim   *Shaa-sawi?* [I don't know.] I don't know what to do.

Kelly   Are you bothered at all that I'm here?

Ibrahim   You?

Kelly   Or is it just the pot?

Ibrahim   I am only thinking about Raya. I am only thinking that this was the one chance / we had to get enough money.

Kelly   You could've read my letters, couldn't you? You didn't even have to reply or whatever, but you could've at least read them.

Ibrahim   I told you how much this meant to me.

Kelly   Yeah, but –

Ibrahim   I offered you something as a gift.

Kelly   I know.

Ibrahim   But what you did –

Kelly   I know, but don't I –

Ibrahim   It told me who you are.

Kelly   Don't I get a second chance?

Ibrahim   It told me enough.

Faiza   *Ibraheem, kafee. Mo sooch-ha.* [Ibrahim. Stop. It is not her fault.]

Kelly   Maybe it was good I smashed it cos I'm not an arrangement. I'm your daughter? It's not always all about what *you* want.

Ibrahim   It was clear what you wanted.

Kelly   Because I'm a person.

Ibrahim   That is why I have not read your letters.

Kelly   You . . .

Ibrahim   I am very grateful you have come so quickly. But that is everything. You are an arrangement. That is it. You can go now.

Kelly   My flight isn't for five days.

Ibrahim   Then stay, help us, but be quiet.

Faiza   *Ibraheem, shtad-gool elha?* [Ibrahim. What are / you saying to her?]

Ibrahim   Because I have to work and we must see to Raya when we get her back. We will not have time for you.

Kelly   You haven't even told me what happened.

Ibrahim   It is not your business.

Kelly   You just said she was gone.

Faiza   *Leech thaa' jet?* [Why is she upset?]

Ibrahim   *Treed to'roof eesh sar be Raya.* [She wants me to tell her about Raya.]

Faiza   *Goolha. Goolha alla-mood teftihim.* [Tell her then. Tell her about Raya. Then maybe she'll understand why this vase matters, it will explain why we're upset.]

Ibrahim.

Ibrahim   Three weeks ago Raya was taken into a car from outside her school. A friend saw it happen. It was very quick. They knew who she was. They knew where she would come out of her school. They pulled up in a car, and they took her away. Two days later we have a note left on the gate. They know where we live. They think we are rich. And it is so much that they ask for. Fifty thousand dollars. They know this is too much and you do not have to pay them all of it, but near enough. That is why we need this now because we need to pay them so much money.

Kelly   What happens if you can't?

Ibrahim   They leave her body on our doorstep.

Kelly

Ibrahim   Or maybe she is sold. She becomes a prostitute somewhere.

Or they just give her back.

All these things go on. It is how they make money.

Kelly   What about the police?

Ibrahim   They do not have the time. They tell us to pay.

Faiza *clears the food.*

Kelly   *Shokran lekka.* [Thank you.]

Ibrahim *has some more coffee.*

What do you do?

Kelly   Now that everything's –

Ibrahim   I run the museum.

Kelly   Is it open?

Ibrahim   No.

Kelly   Then aren't there more important things?

Ibrahim   For many people the collection is very important.

Kelly   Is it?

Ibrahim   You take it for granted because you have so much. But we want to protect it.

Kelly   Because people steal things?

Ibrahim   Yes.

Kelly   Like what?

Ibrahim   Like –

Kelly   Like old vases?

Ibrahim

Kelly   You can't blame them, can you? I thought that when you saw all those people looting. When it comes down to it, you've got to eat. If you really wanted to help you should go and hand stuff out. Give them something to sell.

Faiza *enters.*

Kelly   Because you spend your life protecting all this stuff but in the end even you, even you'll sell it straight away if you have to look after your daughter. Course you will.

Ibrahim   I have to go.

Ibrahim *stands and picks up the pot.*

Faiza   *Koon hather.* [Be careful.]

Kelly   What happens?

Ibrahim   *Teerga' ellnna insha' allah.* [She will be back with us soon.]

I hope they will not mind . . . what you have done.

He holds the vase.

This is strong glue.

Kelly   Superglue.

Ibrahim   The British make good glue, don't they?

Kelly   Yes.

Ibrahim   Because they are always breaking things.

He leaves.

Scene Two

Raya *enters. She is wearing white clothes, but they are old and dirty. She has a bruise on her face.*

Raya   Once there was a piper. He came to a village which had many rats and he said, I can take them all away for one thousand gold pieces. The people of the village said, yes we will give you anything to take the rats away. So the piper played his pipe and the rats all followed him and were taken away from the village. The people of the village celebrated that the rats had gone. They celebrated all night.

A week later the piper came back and asked for his thousand gold pieces. But the people of the village could not pay the money. They had nothing, because the rats had eaten all their food, and no one had been coming to the village. The people were too poor and they had not thought of how they would pay the piper. So the piper took his revenge. And he played the pipe and all the children of the village came out and followed him. The piper took all the children from the village away for ever. Except for one boy, who could not keep up as he had a bad leg. He came back to the village and told them.

You will never see your children again.

You will never see your children again.

Scene Three

Ibrahim *stands with his bag.*

Kelly *watches from the doorway. He has not seen her.*

Ibrahim *takes his jacket off and sits down at the table.*

He unpacks the bag.

He takes out the vase and puts it on the table.

Kelly   What happened?

Ibrahim   I thought you were asleep.

Kelly   You said you had a buyer arranged.

Ibrahim   Yes.

Kelly   Didn't he want it?

Was it the glue?

We can just smash it up again. Scrape it off, you know? Can't be that difficult.

Or I was thinking, if it's not enough, I'll go home get an appeal going or something. Raise awareness for my little Iraqi sister who's been kidnapped. I'll go on the news. If we do it quickly, we can get people to notice. Give some money. Happens all the time. Could do it in a week.

Ibrahim   It was not the glue.

Kelly   What then?

What did he say?

Ibrahim   Can you give me a moment?

Kelly

Ibrahim   And can you get me some water, please?

Kelly *goes and gets* **Ibrahim** *a glass of water. She puts it down and sits at the table.*

He drinks.

Kelly   What went wrong?

Ibrahim   We will talk in the morning.

Kelly   I won't sleep. So –

Ibrahim   I must discuss this.

Kelly   Go on then.

Ibrahim   With Faiza.

Kelly   Discuss / what?

Ibrahim   Please. Go to bed.

Kelly No.

Ibrahim You don't stop asking questions.

Kelly No, I don't.

Ibrahim Why?

Why are you asking?

Why do you want to know?

Kelly I've got a right to know.

Ibrahim A right?

Kelly

Ibrahim You have no right to know about my family.

Kelly She's my sister.

Ibrahim And I'm your father.

Kelly Apparently.

Ibrahim You should trust me that I will do the right thing. But you don't. Do you?

Kelly

Ibrahim You think you know better. You have not been here a day yet. What makes you think you will know better than me?

Kelly Maybe I don't trust you. Not hard to work out why, is it?

Ibrahim You suspect I am making a mistake of some kind.

Don't you?

Really.

If we are talking the truth.

Kelly The pot's not sold. Yeah, maybe you are.

Ibrahim What makes you think what I am doing is a mistake?

Kelly   You're that kind of man.

Ibrahim   Weak.

Kelly   Careless.

Ibrahim   And why do you think I am *careless?*

Kelly

Ibrahim   I will tell you.

Kelly   Yeah, all right then, tell me what I think.

Ibrahim   You come here and you see this city and you see me and my normal house. You see how poor we are and we don't have the things you have. And you see on your news how the country is fighting itself. And you think we are *all* careless. No, not just careless, you think we are stupid. So this is why you're asking what is going on, because you want to make sure that I am being civilised in what I am doing. That I am being intelligent – *reasonable* in how I am behaving. Because we Iraqis, you think, we tend to get things wrong all the time.

We allow our girls to be kidnapped.

We tend to mess things up.

That is really why you do not trust me.

Kelly   Cos I'm a racist.

Ibrahim   Because you are English. And you don't know any better. When you are a child in England you are still taught underneath that you should rule the world. How in the end Britain has always made the world better.

Kelly   You told me I'm half Iraqi.

Ibrahim   I hoped you were.

Kelly   I am. Whether I like it not. I can't choose.

Ibrahim   Yes, you can. You can choose where you belong.

Kelly   Anyway that's rubbish I don't give a shit about Britain or England or whatever it's none of that it's just that you owe it to me cos it's cost me a lot of time a lot of money to bring this pot here. Now it's just sat on the table. Looks nice but that's not the point is it?

You're just sat here.

Ibrahim

Kelly   And she's waiting.

Ibrahim

Kelly   She's waiting and you're drinking a glass of water. So what's going on?

Ibrahim

Kelly   Unfortunately for you I'll keep asking, cos actually I'm not very English, I've got a big mouth, you said I got it from you, so you've got to put up with it. I've got years of practice answering back saying what I want.

So where have you been where have you been?

What happened?

Where have you been?

Ibrahim   Your mother was right.

Kelly   What did she say?

Ibrahim   That you never shut up.

Kelly   Did she?

Ibrahim   Yes.

Kelly   Please. Dad.

Ibrahim   You must try to understand.

Kelly   Yeah I will, but –

Ibrahim   You must listen.

Kelly

Ibrahim   I left here. I started to drive to my friend who is
going to buy this vase. And . . . Faiza and I, we have disagreed
about this. We have argued but we have . . . I know I must sell
it tonight. I have told Faiza I will. But on my way in the car
I passed all the houses and the lights were on. I stopped the car
and I sat and thought about these families. These children.

Kelly   Thought what?

Ibrahim   Then I came back.

Kelly   All that while your daughter's being beaten up or
tortured.

Ibrahim   Or something worse than that, I am sure.

Kelly

Ibrahim   You don't know what they do to some of the girls.

Kelly

Ibrahim   So do you see?

Kelly   You can get the money to pay for her. You said it
yourself, everyone does it. That's what people do.

Ibrahim   Yes.

Kelly   That's what the police tell you to do.

Ibrahim   This is what people do, yes.

Kelly   Right.

Ibrahim   They pay.

Kelly   So get on / with it?

Ibrahim   And as they pay things get worse and worse.
Everything gets darker. The country falls apart. My friends are
dead, their children are kidnapped. Our women must cover
themselves. Because people give in. Because no one stands up
and says it has to stop.

Kelly   Except you.

Ibrahim Everything has to start somewhere.

Kelly OK.

Well done.

Ibrahim

Kelly I'm really impressed.

Ibrahim

Kelly You're a real man.

Ibrahim You have not listened.

Kelly What world are you in where you get to be some *hero* you think you're going to sort it all out – sort out your country with this yeah? Yeah maybe you will maybe you'll suddenly get everyone to change what they're doing and forget their families and think of their country. Maybe you'll *inspire* them all.

Good luck, cos that's not going to happen? But you're going to leave your daughter raped and killed and you're going to know you've done the wrong thing for the rest of your life because it'll be obvious that it hasn't made any difference. So be a doctor or something if you want to be important. Join Oxfam? But make sure you sell the fucking pot first, yeah?

Ibrahim It is all about these small ways.

Every time that things have changed it is through someone saying no. If ten families in a row do not pay, they will stop.

Kelly If.

Ibrahim And this will be difficult for you, but listen. Listen and think. Sometimes if something is right we have to be ready to die. We have to be ready to sacrifice our sons and our daughters for what we believe.

Kelly That sounds like a terrorist.

Ibrahim No, I am not a terrorist, but if we are not as strong as them they will win.

Kelly   You're just doing the same thing again. Leaving another daughter. Putting an *idea* first.

Ibrahim   No.

Kelly   As I grew up, when bad things happened I used to hide under the blankets and I'd ask God for my dad to turn up that night and protect me. Look after us.

Ibrahim   We are not talking about you.

Kelly   But he never did.

Ibrahim   You want me to exchange my daughter for someone else's.

Kelly   That's what father's *do.*

Dad.

That's what they *do.*

They look after their own.

Ibrahim   Maybe your fathers do that. But important men, better men, look after everyone. They look after their country.

Faiza *enters.*

Ibrahim   They stick to what they believe.

She sees the vase.

Looks at **Ibrahim**.

Ibrahim   *Ma'rah asawehha. Min fathelek.* [No. I won't do it. So please –]

Faiza   *Mo akhathna 'karrar.* [We made a decision.]

Ibrahim   *La ma abee.* [I don't –]

Faiza   *Akhathna al-karrar soowa.* [We made a decision together.]

Ibrahim   *Chan mo saah.* [It was wrong.]

Faiza   *Bee 'ahha.* [Sell it.]

Kelly What's she saying?

Faiza *Wallah atrookak. Inta andeck mas'ooleeia itejah bintak wa aa'eelta.* [I will leave. You will never see me again. You have a duty to me and your daughter and your family.]

Ibrahim *Let-hadeed-en-eee.* [Don't threaten me.]

Kelly She agrees with me.

Ibrahim *Let-hadeed-en-eee.* [Don't threaten me.]

Kelly *takes* **Faiza***'s hand.*

Ibrahim She is a mother. It is for mothers to care. But it is for fathers to act. For everyone. To be responsible.

He sits.

La' La'. [No. No.]

I'm not going to sell it. She knows the sort of man I am.

Kelly You're not even looking at her now.

I am.

And she's been crying.

Faiza *Shloon day a'nid.* [Look how stubborn he is.]

Kelly I don't think she trusts you.

Faiza *Rah ammalah. Hayetrokha lell-moat.* [He has given up on her. Left her for dead. He is stupid.]

Kelly *picks up* **Ibrahim***'s car keys from the table.*

Kelly We'll go.

Take the car.

The . . . *sayarra?* [Car.]

Take it ourselves. Us. *Nahno.* [Us.]

Ibrahim Go to bed. Both of you.

Rooho na-mo. [Go and sleep.]

Na-mo. [Sleep!]

Kelly   Faiza. We'll go. Us. *Nahno. Na'am.* [Us. Yes?]

Yella. [Come on.]

Faiza *looks at* **Ibrahim**.

She goes to him and hits him.

He barely moves.

Then **Faiza** *leaves.*

Kelly *waits.*

She doesn't know what to do.

Kelly   Where's she gone?

Ibrahim *sits.*

Kelly *stares at him.*

Kelly   Maybe all Iraqis are stupid.

Ibrahim   What?

Kelly   Maybe all Iraqis are stupid. They put Saddam Hussein in charge for twenty years let him kill thousands of people didn't do anything about it. And in the end when we do get rid of him, they just start fighting each other when all the time if they just sorted themselves out they could get a country together. Cos you've got all that oil. You could be rich, yeah? You know that's what a lot of people in Britain think? That you're immature as a people. You're medieval. All the time you're proving yourself not clever enough, not civilised enough to even run an army, a police force or a government. You're all corrupt. There are lots of people in Britain who want to say – grow up. And if they were here now they would look at you and they wouldn't understand why you're just sat at home, not looking after your daughter.

You're putting an idea first. Like everyone here. Blowing people up for ideas. Killing women.

You're stupid.

That's the only reason I can think that you've come back
without her.

Ibrahim   In the morning I will take you to the airport and
you will go.

Faiza *comes back in with her coat on. She picks up the keys, takes the
vase.*

Faiza   *Whaeen ala'anwan?* [Where is the address?]

Ibrahim   *Inti* – [You –]

Faiza   *Marah twagoofni. He-yeah saah. Itha inta matrooh. Ini, arooh.*
[You won't stop me. She is right. If you won't go I have to.
Where is it?]

Ibrahim   *Al'anwan bil sayarra.* [In the car.]

Faiza *turns to go.*

Kelly   I'll come with you.

Faiza   No. Thank you.

Kelly   No, I will. I'll come with you.

She doesn't understand this. Your friends won't either. They'll
think you were stupid.

You'll lose your wife. You'll lose everything.

Ibrahim

Faiza *makes to go.*

Kelly   Wait.

Dad. Last chance cos we're going.

Last chance.

Stand up.

Part Three

Scene One

Kelly *is sorting through her things, putting some in bin-liners, others in boxes.*

Susan *watches.* **Kelly** *hasn't seen her. They both have cups of tea.*

When **Susan** *speaks,* **Kelly** *doesn't seem to hear.*

Susan I remember you had wanted to go by train, but I insisted on driving you and helping you in with your things. I hadn't been to Sheffield before. We saw those huge towers by the side of the M1, do you remember? As we came down the slip road I thought I was taking you down, at the age of eighteen, into a northern hell where you'd binge-drink, smoke drugs and have lots and lots of very bad, unprotected, sex.

Because that's what I did when I was eighteen.

But you aren't like me any more are you?

I remember when you were little you used to follow me round the house as I cleaned, copying everything I did. You never clean now.

We got to the halls and I helped you get all your stuff in. All the other parents were doing it, but you wanted me to leave. You were embarrassed. I had this heavy box, full of books, and I got up the stairs and went into this little room, in the flat you were sharing with six strangers. I could hear them next door laughing. I put the box down on the bed and opened it. I thought I would help you unpack. And at the top of this box I'd opened was a photo of your father, with another woman and a girl.

You came in and found me looking at the photo, with the box open.

'It's all right, Mum,' you said. 'I'll unpack, you can go back home if you want.'

'If you want.'

I said I had to get back anyway. You kissed me. We hugged.
I cried. Then I apologised. I could see it embarrassed you. It's
a long drive from Sheffield to London, and by the time I got
home I had stopped at three service stations, kept on having to
dry my eyes. It was dangerous.

And you stayed at university the whole year. Came home for
Christmas, in the end. But you were happier there, weren't
you? Happier away.

Kelly Mum . . .

Susan Yes?

Kelly *holds up a tennis racket.*

Kelly Do you want this? I've got a new one.

Susan Yes.

Yes I do.

Kelly Right.

Susan The last couple of years have been the same. We see
each other now and again. Sometimes I tell you I'm unhappy.
You said I should try to meet someone. I had no real reason
to feel lonely. I was lucky, you said, living here. I had no idea.
You thought I was moaning.

But we used to be friends.

I should never have told you how I felt. It made you feel guilty.
So you stayed away more.

Kelly *holds up a big old CD Walkman.*

Kelly How were you supposed to go running with this
strapped to your leg? It's massive. Do you want it? It's ancient.

Susan It was a birthday present.

Kelly When?

Susan Don't you remember?

Kelly   No.

Susan   You said it was what you wanted.

Kelly   Did I?

Susan   It was expensive.

Kelly   Doesn't look it.

Susan   For us. At the time.

Kelly   Well, I've got an iPod. You can have it if you want.

Susan   Yes. Thanks. Keep it.

I came to the graduation, but I wasn't sure what to do. You seemed to be having so much fun, and I was standing at the side of it all. All the other parents seemed to know each other. You didn't introduce me.

You moved differently now. And you spoke like them.

I didn't recognise you.

Kelly   You all right, Mum?

Susan   Yes. Of course.

Kelly   You're staring again.

Susan   Am I?

Kelly   Gone zombie.

Susan   Sorry.

Kelly   Just a bit weird, you're like . . .

She does an impression.

Susan   Having a think.

Kelly   Yeah. Good. Keep it working. Don't want you going mental.

Susan   No.

Kelly   Don't want to put you in a home.

Susan No.

Kelly Not yet.

Susan *stares again.*

Kelly You sure you're all right?

Susan Yes.

Kelly But you would always say that, wouldn't you?
To me. Even if you're not.

Susan What time do you have to be there?

Kelly Half-one. Under the clock.

Susan It must be strange.

Kelly I've got to go, haven't I?

Susan No. You really don't.

Kelly

Susan What are you going to do?

Kelly London Eye. Shopping. Houses of Parliament.

Susan Then what?

Kelly That's it. Then back on the train to Paris. It's just a day trip apparently.

Susan So we're still on for tomorrow.

Kelly Yeah.

Susan You and me?

Kelly Yeah, why?

Susan Thought you'd forgotten.

Kelly What do you mean?

Susan You're leaving on Sunday.

Kelly   I know.

Susan   And you've only just got back.

Kelly   I told you . . .

Susan   And now you're packing everything up. Throwing it away.

Kelly   It's what young people do. Everyone else's parents are proud. They're pleased their kids have got jobs. Making a start. But you . . .

Susan   I'm pleased.

Kelly   Cos you go to uni. Leave. If you're lucky, you get a job. Have a life. La la. It's what we're supposed to do.

Susan   I miss having you around.

Kelly   We always used to shout at each other.

Susan *smiles.*

Susan   I know.

I'm quieter these days.

Kelly   So am I.

Susan   Don't like it.

Kelly   Why not?

Susan   People change.

Kelly   That's good.

Susan   No.

You will be careful today.

Kelly   Yes.

Susan   Don't get upset.

Kelly   I won't.

Susan   You've got nothing to prove.

Kelly   Do you want a wooden spoon?

Susan   Nothing to say. If you don't want to.

Kelly   Mum?

Susan   What?

Kelly   Spoon?

Susan   Kelly. Anything.

Anything of yours you don't want, put down there, and I'll have it.

If you're going.

Cos I don't know when you'll come back, do I?

Kelly   Stop it.

Susan   Remember I'm here.

Kelly   Mum.

Come on.

You just need to move on. Everyone else has.

Susan   I know. What are you going to do with that?

Kelly   Every time I've done a sort-out like this you go through before you throw it away, don't you?

To check.

You hate me throwing things away.

Susan   Yes.

I worry you'll forget.

Because these things.

They're part of who you are, aren't they?

Scene Two

The room in darkness. **Ibrahim** *sits in a chair in Baghdad.*

Although it is only three years later, he looks even older. He moves less and the light has gone out of his eyes.

He is ill.

Ibrahim   I want to tell you what has happened.

They say it is getting better now.

The Americans are leaving Baghdad. The British have left Basra. They say things are better. The number of attacks has gone down. They say that Iraqi forces have control. It will all be all right now.

This is a lie. Gangs still kidnap children, militia kill women. The Americans and British have not left because things are better. They have left because things are getting worse. They know many more people are about to die and they do not want the responsibility.

We reopen the museum tomorrow. Not because it is safe. Not because it is ready. But because things have to be seen to be getting better. We have been ordered to. It is like that everywhere. We are covering things up. We are making it seem like it is good. But underneath feelings are just as strong. And they will not go away.

This country has been broken into pieces and people are grabbing what they can. They are preparing for an even larger war. And when it comes, I think everyone will just look out for themselves. But no one will win, and the pieces of this country will become dust. The buildings will be destroyed. The museums will be emptied and the children will die. Iran and Syria and Turkey will get involved. It will become hell. It has all happened before elsewhere. India, Africa, Israel. Whenever the Americans and the British invade, fight, give up and go home.

I wanted to tell you all this because I hope you will understand now why I did not want to sell the vase.

I hope maybe you will see that sometimes other things are important.

Faiza left Baghdad a few months after you were here. I have not spoken to her since. She had some family in the south and they helped her to make a new start. Sometimes she writes and tells me how things are. She does not talk about the past. Perhaps she has forgotten. I have not seen her for three years. And I miss Raya. I miss her too.

And I know you want the truth. So I am sorry, I must tell you that I have tried, but I cannot forgive you. Not now. But if you write back, I will read it this time. I promise you that.

Because we both have to learn to listen, don't we?

Scene Three

The museum.

On a stand are the broken pieces of the vase.

Raya *and* **Kelly** *stand on either side of it.*

Raya   History.

Kelly   Yeah?

Raya   Yes.

Kelly   Boring.

Raya   Not for me.

Kelly   We're in the right place then.

Raya   Yes.

Kelly   Never liked it. Too dry. Too much to get your head round.

Raya   And we've got more than you.

Kelly   More?

Raya   More history.

Kelly   Yeah I suppose you do. You win. Well done.

Raya

Kelly   When are you going?

Raya   In a few months.

Kelly   In Baghdad.

Raya   Yes.

Kelly   It's still open?

Raya   Yes. But I wanted to travel first.

Kelly   How can you afford it?

Raya   My uncle. He said he would pay. He is making money.

Kelly   How?

Raya   I don't ask.

Kelly   What do you think of London?

Raya   It is like I was told it would be.

Kelly   What were you told?

Raya   There are people on the streets begging. But no one gives them money.

Kelly   Yeah, they spend it on drugs.

Raya   How do you know?

Kelly   We give it to charities instead?

Raya   Do you?

Kelly   People do. I don't have enough. I'm a student.

Raya   You are well dressed.

Kelly   Yeah?

Raya   You look very nice.

Kelly   Thank you.

Raya   I think you have enough.

Kelly   I just want to have a good time, yeah?

I thought once we've done this we'll go on the London Eye, you know, the wheel? Then we'll go to Parliament like you wanted to. And I thought we might go shopping? / Does that sound –

Raya   I don't mind.

Kelly   Good.

Raya   Have you come and seen this before?

Kelly   This?

I didn't even know it was here.

Raya   You didn't look.

Kelly

Raya   'A calcite vase from Mesopotamia, in three parts. Early Dynastic III, about 2600 BC. Grave PG-337. Believed lost from the National Museum of Iraq after the invasion by coalition forces in 2003. Recovered from a dealer a year ago, and held in trust by the British Museum on indefinite loan.'

It's smaller than he described it.

Kelly   Do you see much of him?

Raya   We have started to write to each other now. I think it is important we do. I am learning a lot.

Kelly   How is he?

Raya   Lonely.

Kelly   He sent me a letter too.

Raya   Did he?

Kelly

Raya   He did not tell me.

Kelly   No?

Raya   What did he say?

Kelly   That there's no hope.

Raya   He is right.

Kelly   Then why go to university there? Why don't you get out? You could come here. Stay with me or something.

Raya   I would never live here.

Kelly   Don't mention it.

Raya   And if there is a war I want to be at home.

Kelly   Why?

Raya   To protect the country.

Kelly   To fight?

Raya   If I have to.

Kelly   You sound like Dad.

Raya   Good.

Kelly   We saved your life.

Raya   Yes.

Kelly   So don't waste it, yeah?

Raya   Tell me what happened with this.

Kelly   What do you mean?

Raya   When you brought this vase back. I hear from my mother that one thing happened and then our father writes and tells me it was different. But you were there. What did you do?

Kelly   Me and your mum tried to persuade Dad to sell it. But he didn't do anything. Wouldn't change his mind. So we took the vase and said we'd do it ourselves. When we were about to drive off he stopped us. He sold the vase, got the money and got you back.

Raya   Then my mother left anyway.

Kelly   Yeah.

Maybe she couldn't trust him after that.

Raya   She didn't try.

Kelly   That's not fair.

Raya   She shouldn't have left. He was trying to do the right thing.

Kelly   What happened to you?

Raya

Kelly   What was it like?

Raya   Does it matter?

Kelly

Raya   It was the wrong decision.

Kelly   To get you back.

Raya   To pay them. They did not deserve it.

Kelly   What do you mean?

Raya   It is not important that I am alive.

Kelly   You think?

Raya   Many of my friends have lost brothers and sisters. We have grown up with our country at war, and we have been poor and we have had nothing. It is all falling apart. But we all have to take responsibility for what we have done.

Other children were killed because you made him sell the vase.

Kelly   Shut up.

Raya   I wish he had been stronger.

I wish you had not been there.

Kelly   We did what we thought was right.

Raya   You came to Baghdad and straight away you were telling us what to do. You shouted. You didn't listen. You didn't know anything. And look at it now. Look at it.

Kelly   Then I'm sorry. We didn't just leave you to –

Raya   This vase that meant so much to Dad is in here. In London. Can I have your bag?

Kelly   Why?

Raya   We are going to put these pieces in the bag and you will take them out.

Kelly   We're –

No.

Raya   We're going to steal them.

Kelly

Raya   Then I will take them back and put them in the museum in Baghdad.

Kelly   There's alarms.

Raya   Where they should be.

Kelly   I'm not doing anything.

Raya   It will help for you to say sorry to me.

Kelly   I'm not.

Raya   To my father. To your family.

Kelly   I'm not sorry.

Raya   You should be.

Kelly   There's guards. They'll arrest you.

Raya   Then I'll tell them. When they ask what we're doing, I'll tell them we're taking it home.

Kelly   Does Dad know?

Raya   Give me your bag.

Kelly He doesn't, does he? I thought we were going to meet, have some coffee or something, get to know each other, I don't want this.

Raya He is right in what he says about you.

Kelly What does he say?

Raya That you have quick thoughts, not long ones.

Kelly Don't know what that means.

Raya You think of the next minute. Of those people who happen to be around you. You cannot imagine anything bigger.

Kelly I tried so hard to be part of your family. I went all the way to Baghdad. I used all the money I'd saved when I could've travelled the world to deliver this back and when I got there . . . Dad hated me. We haven't spoken since . . . but then you said you were coming and he wrote and I thought –

Raya You thought maybe it was over?

Kelly That we could make a new start. Yes.

Raya It's not over. Have you replied to him?

Kelly Yeah. I was going to.

Raya This will be your reply. He is not interested in what you say any more. It is what you do.

Kelly How do you know what he wants?

Raya I know him.

Kelly So do I.

Raya I grew up with him.

Kelly

Raya

Kelly He said if I write he'll read it.

Raya If I come home with this, he will know you care.

You have to work hard to be a good daughter.

Kelly   Yeah.

Raya   Yeah.

Kelly   I didn't ask for any of this.

Raya   Neither did we.

Kelly   I'm not stealing anything, and you're not having my bag. If you want to go for coffee and hang out and stuff then fine, but I'm not waiting around while you do this. I've had enough. If this is what you're going to do, I'll just go home now and that's it. Yeah? I won't write, I won't call again. You can tell him when you get back. I've had it.

Raya   You'll go shopping and not care.

Kelly   Yes. I'll go shopping and not care.

Raya   Like everyone else.

Kelly   Like everyone else. Not my fault.

Raya   Are you sure?

Kelly   Yeah.

Raya   I feel sorry for you.

Kelly   Don't.

Raya   You have nothing to fight for.

Kelly   Yeah. I'm lucky. I'm British. I don't need to fight.

Raya   It is important to have something you would die for.

Kelly   My mum.

Raya   Anything else?

Kelly   No.

Raya   Then what are doing in your life? What are you living for?

Kelly

Raya   I think you're right.

I don't think we'll see each other again.

Kelly   Maybe it's for the best.

Raya   Yeah.

They look at each other.

So you are leaving?

Kelly   Yeah. Going shopping. You coming?

Raya   No.

I have to do this.

Kelly   I can't deal with it.

Raya   I know.

Kelly *puts her coat on.*

Picks up her bag.

Kelly   Fine.

I'll leave you here. I'll walk down the corridor and end up in the big square of the British Museum that's covered in glass. It'll be really bright. Then I'll walk out and look back at this massive building, and maybe notice that no one here is actually British. This is the British Museum but everyone is a tourist. All the countries in the world come here and look at all this stuff except this one. Cos maybe we've got better things to do.

Raya *takes the vase pieces and puts them in the bag and walks away.*

Kelly   Then I'll walk out of the gates and go down towards Covent Garden. And it'll be strange. Because I'll know, somehow I'll know for sure that I'm never going to hear from you again. I won't need to have anything more to do with it all.

Iraq. Dad. You. Faiza. And I should feel guilty. I should feel upset and worried and like I've let you down. But I won't. I'll feel lighter. I'll feel happy. Normal. Because I can't do anything about it all, and all it was doing was making me feel worse and worse. But now . . . it'll be . . . gone. And I can be me.

I'll look in the shop windows at the clothes, and Sarah will text me and I'll call her back and we'll decide we're going to go to Koko tonight with Steve and the others, so I reckon I want to treat myself, buy something proper nice. And I'll go through these glass doors and a woman will offer to help me and I'll be shopping and I'll be feeling great. I will feel so fucking normal. Shopping and eating and coffee and out and home.

It'll be bright and it'll be happy and it'll be easy.

And I won't need to worry.

Just me.

Just as I want it.

Just as it should be.

Printed in the USA
CPSIA information can be obtained
at www.ICGtesting.com
LVHW020931171024
794056LV00003B/713

9 781408 106778